Contents

Australia: Unpacked

G'day! You've arrived in awesome Australia, a large landmass in the Pacific Ocean and the sixth largest country in the world. Australia gets its name from the Latin word *australis*, meaning southern, and it's the biggest country found entirely in the southern hemisphere. It's a land of amazing wildlife and astonishing scenery - from dusty outback deserts to tropical forests and spectacular coral reefs. Turn the pages to learn about the country and its people, from an underground town to a tuna tossing festival, and a major city once called Batmania!

Fact file

Area: 7,692,024km²
Population: 23.04 million
Capital city: Canberra
Land Borders: None
Currency: The Australian Dollar

Flag:

The Australian flag was chosen in 1901 from a competition that attracted more than 32,000 entries.

Australia

Useful Phrases

G'day - Hello
Hoo roo - Goodbye
Ripper - That's terrific!
Thongs - Flip-flop sandals
Full as a goog - Totally full up after a meal
No worries - You're welcome or that's fine
Nosebag - Takeaway food

Tucker - Food
Dunnie - The toilet
Drongo - A fool or dimwit

Australian Coat of Arms:

The Australian coat of arms features two native creatures, an emu and a kangaroo. They are said to represent the country moving forwards as the leg structure of each creature stops them from being able to walk backwards.

The largest cattle station in the world is Anna Creek Station in South Australia. At over 34,000km² in size, it is bigger than the country of Belgium!

The Dingo Fence is the longest barricade in the world. The 5,614km fence was built during the 1880s to protect sheep in the south-eastern parts of Australia from dingoes (wild dogs).

Exploration and Discovery

Aboriginal peoples have lived in Australia for tens of thousands of years - long before people from other parts of the world discovered it. European explorers had long talked about whether 'Terra Australis' (a southern land) existed. Dutch, and later British, sailors discovered it did!

Early Exploration

In 1606, the *Duyfken*, a ship captained by Dutchman Willem Janszoon landed at the northernmost tip of Australia, the Cape York Peninsula. Abel Tasman discovered what he named Van Diemen's Land, now called Tasmania, in 1642. Captain James Cook of the *Endeavour* sailed from England in 1768 and landed at Botany Bay (near present day Sydney) in 1770. He charted much of Australia's eastern coast and claimed it for Britain.

Captain Cook's statue in Sydney (right) and a replica of his ship, the *Endeavour* (above).

Early Colonies

The British first used Australia as a giant prison, sending 162,000 prisoners there between 1788 and 1868. Convicts had to endure a terrible journey, often chained below deck for months in horrid conditions. Many didn't arrive alive. Those that did were used as a source of cheap labour to build settlements and they faced severe punishments. One man was whipped 500 times just for stealing a pumpkin!

The remains of the Port Arthur prison colony on Tasmania which opened in 1833.

NO WAY!

Australia's first ever police force, the Night Watch, was made up of a dozen of the best behaved convicts at the first colony.

Exploring the Interior

From the 1800s, free settlers also arrived and started exploring further inland. In 1860, the Burke and Wills expedition set off from Melbourne on camels intent on crossing Australia from south to north. Despite carrying ludicrous amounts of kit – including a Chinese dinner gong, dandruff combs and a bathtub – they got close. However, all but one of the party perished.

Burke and Wills struggle back to Cooper Creek after trekking deep into northern Australia.

City Sights

Work began building Australia's capital city, Canberra, in 1913. It is now the seat of Australia's government and home to around 370,000 people. It is nicknamed 'the bush capital' as it was built inland in a dry area of bushland. Canberra is Australia's eighth largest city as bigger settlements have developed mostly along the country's enormous coastline.

Super Sydney

Sydney is Australia's most visited and biggest city with more than 4.6 million people living in it or nearby. It sprawls outwards from its giant harbour area. It is the financial and business centre of the country and boasts hundreds of attractions including the world-famous Sydney Opera House and the Harbour Bridge. George Street is Australia's oldest road but is now packed with towering skyscrapers along much of its length.

The majestic Sydney Opera House was completed in 1973 and boasts over 1.05 million roof tiles.

Melbourne's Flinders Street railway station lies on the bank of the Yarra River.

Perfect Perth

Western Australia covers an area of over 2.5 million km^2 – around a third of the country – yet is home to only 2.4 million people. More than three quarters of these live in and around the city of Perth. Founded in 1829, Perth lies on the Swan River. The city is bathed in sunshine most of the year. The heat is tempered by a cool afternoon wind, known as the Freemantle Doctor, that comes off the Indian Ocean.

Perth's waterfront close to Kings Park – one of the world's biggest city parks at 4km^2.

Marvellous Melbourne

Melbourne was originally called Batmania! It was named after one of its founders, John Batman. The city lies on a large natural harbour called Port Phillip Bay and grew quickly after gold was discovered in the mid-19th century. A major centre of culture, music and art in Australia, the city also has the largest tram network in the world.

NO WAY!

Perth is actually closer to Jakarta in Indonesia than it is to the Australian cities of Sydney and Canberra.

Not All Desert

Much of the centre of Australia is hot and dry with deserts such as the Great Victoria Desert and the Great Sandy Desert. Each of these is larger than the whole of the UK. However, the land is also varied and includes grasslands, mountains, wetlands and lush rainforests. There are large areas of dry scrubland known as 'the bush'.

NO WAY!

Over 100 years ago, Mount Kosciuszko was found to be shorter in height than its neighbour, Mount Townsend. So, the authorities switched the names of the mountains round!

Water from the Murray River is used in irrigating vineyards and fruit orchards.

Forests and Rivers

Northern and eastern Australia have tropical climates and parts receive well over 1,000mm of rainfall each year. Northern Queensland sometimes receives more than 4,000mm. Large, lush rainforests and wetlands often exist in these areas providing homes for a great range of creatures. Australia doesn't have many rivers or lakes but its largest is the 2,508km-long Murray River. Together with the Darling River, which flows into it, these rivers drain a big part of southeastern Australia.

Uluru

Australia's biggest natural icon is a massive rocky outcrop found in the centre of the country. An Australian icon, it was first named Ayers Rock but is now known by its local aboriginal name of Uluru. Made of red sandstone, Uluru rises 345m high above the surrounding land and it's a 9.4km walk around its base. Visitors are asked not to climb Uluru as it is sacred to the local peoples.

Uluru is over 460km from the town of Alice Springs by road, but it has an airport just 8km away.

Hills and Mountains

Much of Australia is flat or made up of rolling plains, but the country does have a number of mountain ranges. These include the Blue Mountains and the Great Dividing Range. The country's highest point, the 2,228m-high Mount Kosciuszko, is in the Snowy Mountains. High slopes mean winter sports and ski resorts, such as Thredbo and Mt Buller, receive enough snowfall in the winter months to attract thousands of winter sports enthusiasts.

The Three Sisters rock formation is found in the Blue Mountains.

Aussie Animals

More than 85% of all Australia's reptiles, insects and fish are endemic, meaning they are only found in the wild in Australia. There are few land predators like wolves, lions and leopards and, partly as a result, a wide range of wildlife has flourished.

Marsupials are mammals that give birth to live young that are not fully-developed and live for a time inside their mother's pouch. Koalas, wallabies, kangaroos and wombats are all marsupials. The largest marsupial is the red kangaroo, which can stand up to 2m tall and hops at speeds of up to 40km/h!

Koala

Giant salt-water crocodiles, up to 7m long, patrol the coastal waters of northern Australia.

A wombat's droppings are cube-shaped. They use their flat-sided poos to mark the boundaries of their territory.

Australia is home to a number of deadly dangerous creatures from the highly poisonous funnel-web and redback spiders to the world's most venomous snake, the inland Taipan.

Redback spider

Monotremes are the only mammals in the world that lay eggs. They are only found in New Guinea and Australia and include the echidna and the duck-billed platypus.

Echidna

Box jellyfish float around the quieter shores. One can kill a human in minutes if enough of its tentacles sting at the same time!

More than 800 species of bird, including the noisy kookaburra and the 2m-tall giant emu, live in Australia.

Kookaburra

Long-Distance Travellers

Australia is huge. It's approximately 4,000km wide and 3,800km from south to north. The UK would fit about 32 times inside its area! To get around, Australians rely on land and air transport and settle in for long journeys to cover the huge distances to reach their destinations.

NO WAY!

In 2006, the world's longest ever road train consisting of 112 trailers drove a short distance through Clifton, Queensland. The truck and trailers measured over 1.4km in length!

Road and Rail Trains

Australia has over 41,000km of railway lines. Many link towns within a single region but there are two services that cross the country – the Indian Pacific (east-west) and the Ghan (north-south). A return journey on the Indian Pacific railway could take over 130 hours! There's also another kind of train operating in Australia – road trains. These are powerful trucks hauling two, three or more massive trailers carrying livestock, raw materials or finished goods long distances.

A road train powered by a big rig truck trundles across Australia's Northern Territory.

Air Today

With such big distances between major cities, many Australians take to the air to visit friends and relatives elsewhere in the country. Australia has over 300 airports with paved runways and hundreds more rougher airstrips. The Royal Flying Doctor Service operates from 21 airfields around Australia bringing medical expertise to out of the way areas and treating over 270,000 patients per year. And spare a thought for the postal service in northern Australia which performs a regular Cairns to Cape York airmail service, travelling 1,450km a day!

One of the Royal Flying Doctor Service's 60+ aircraft. The service made 74,000 flights in 2012.

Road signs warn drivers of wild animals crossing the road!

Roadside Attractions

Dotted along Australia's roads are more than 100 giant objects, from a 6m-high model of Australian criminal, Ned Kelly, to giant fruit, vegetables and animals. Famous 'Big Things' include the Big Prawn at Ballina, the Big Lobster at Kingston and the Big Guitar at Tamworth, the country music capital of Australia. The first big thing, the 11m-long concrete Big Banana, at Coffs Harbour, was unveiled in 1964 as a roadside attraction to make drivers stop at a roadside banana stall.

The 16m-high Big Pineapple in Nambour has wowed roadside travellers since 1971.

Go, Aussie, Go!

Australians love the great outdoors and take advantage of the good weather and vast spaces to play a wide range of sports. Despite being a small country by population, Australians punch well above their weight in global sporting events providing world champions in many sports from athletics to motorsports. The country has also hosted the Olympics twice (Melbourne, 1956, and Sydney, 2000) and won 468 Olympic medals since 1896.

The mighty MCG holds 100,000 spectators and is used for cricket and Aussie Rules.

Howzat!

Australians love their cricket. The first recorded game occurred in Sydney in 1803 and tours to England began 75 years later. Each of the six states of Australia supply a team that competes in the Sheffield Shield each year. The national cricket team's fiercest rivalry is with England in the Ashes series usually held every two years. It's an Australian tradition for a five-day Test match to start on Boxing Day every year at the Melbourne Cricket Ground (MCG).

Aussie Rules

Invented in Melbourne, Australian Rules Football is hugely popular with more than half a million players. Top teams like Essendon, Carlton and Collingwood are supported by thousands of fans. Teams of 18 players a side move the ball up a giant pitch looking to kick a goal between two tall posts. Leaping, tackling and catching make it an all-action contact sport.

NO WAY!

The Socceroos, Australia's national football team, are the world record holders for the biggest scoreline in international football – a 31-0 thrashing of American Samoa in 2001.

Collingwood and Essendon players battle for the ball during a fierce Aussie Rules game.

Surf's up at Snappers Point on the Gold Coast, south of the city of Brisbane.

Surf's Up

With thousands of kilometres of coast, it's no surprise that Australians excel in water sports. Australian swimmers, such as Ian Thorpe and Libby Trickett, have swept all before them, whilst Australia boasts a fierce rivalry with the US in sailing competitions like the America's Cup. Australia has many world-class surfing spots including Noosa Heads, Bells Beach and Snapper Rocks. Competitions attract the world's top surfers.

Mine Time

Mining makes more money for Australia than either the farming or manufacturing industries. It is the world's biggest exporter of coal, mining 405 million tonnes in 2010-11, and contains almost a quarter of the entire world's known supplies of uranium. In 2013, massive deposits of oil in shale were announced in the Australian outback, which may further increase the country's reliance on minerals for its wealth.

Trucks are dwarfed by the huge Super Pit gold mine.

Metals Mining

Australia is one of the world's biggest producers of iron ore, nickel, copper, aluminium, manganese and zinc – all metals used heavily in industry. Many of these need plenty of workers to recover and process them which has seen mining settlements become towns, such as Broken Hill and Karratha. Much of the metal is exported to other countries particularly those in Asia but also further afield. Just over half of all the money Australia receives from exports comes from its minerals.

A giant dump truck carts rocky ore from which metals may be recovered.

Coober Pedy's golf course features only rock and sand. Golfers carry a piece of artificial turf with them to play the ball off, whilst the 'greens' are black and made of sand slicked down with oil.

Coober Pedy

Australia has large deposits of precious stones including diamonds and opals. More than 85% of the world's opals are produced here and Coober Pedy in South Australia is a major source. At this unusual settlement many people live underground in old mines or holes in the rock they've cut themselves. There are even underground churches and restaurants, all designed to be cooler than living on the scorching surface.

The Breakaways hill range lies just north of Coober Pedy.

Gold Rush

In 1851, gold was discovered in New South Wales, triggering a massive gold rush. This helped to more than double Australia's 437,000 strong population in less than a decade. Australia is still a major gold producer, one of the five biggest in the world. The biggest open pit gold mine in Australia is the Super Pit in Western Australia. This gigantic hole, 3.5km long, 1.5km wide and 570m deep, is the result of some 15 million tonnes of rock being moved by giant diggers and trucks every year.

On the Coast

Around nine out of ten Australians live within 70km of the coast and it plays a large part in their daily lives. The fishing industry lands tens of thousands of tonnes of prawns, tuna and other fish every year to feed Australians' healthy appetites for seafood. There are over 300 surf lifesaver clubs, whose members patrol around 400 beaches helping to keep visitors safe.

Bondi Beach has a shark net 150m offshore to protect swimmers.

Along the Coast

At 200km long, the Coorong is Australia's longest single beach. In contrast, Bondi Beach is only a kilometre long but, because it is located just minutes from Sydney, it's incredibly popular. Other parts of the coastline are rocky. Many visitors tour the Great Ocean Road to catch spectacular views, including the Twelve Apostles, now just eight limestone stacks. This 243km-long stretch of beautiful highway was built by veterans returning from World War I.

Islands and Territories

Australia's territory includes a staggering 8,200 islands. The largest is Tasmania, home to half a million people most of who live in and around the major city of Hobart. Further north, Fraser Island is the world's largest island made of sand. The 123km-long island is home to lush rainforests, mangrove swamps and over 100 freshwater lakes. One of the farthest flung Australian islands is Christmas Island, lying in the Indian Ocean 2,600km west of Perth. It is famous for its enormous population of around 30 million red crabs that swamp the island.

Red crabs swamp a railway line on Christmas Island. ⬇

Good Reef

The Great Barrier Reef is the world's largest coral reef and the only living structure that can be seen from outer space. It stretches 2,300km off the coast of north-eastern Australia and its network of coral and islands is bigger than the UK and Portugal combined! It provides homes for a dizzying range of wildlife with over 1,600 types of fish and 3,000 different species of molluscs, including the enormous giant clam which can weigh more than 200kg.

NO WAY!

The Great Barrier Reef has its own postbox, more than 70km offshore on a diving platform at Agincourt Reef.

21

Native Australians

Peoples from south-east Asia reached and settled in Australia tens of thousands of years before Europeans. At the time, sea levels were lower and a land bridge may have existed part or most of the way to Australia. Those who settled in Australia developed their own ways of life and beliefs with more than 200 different Aboriginal languages or dialects. Each tribal group had, and many still have, their own territory in which some landmarks are sacred.

NO WAY!

One type of non-returning boomerang used by Aboriginal hunters is called a kylie!

Tools of the Trade

Australian Aboriginals were traditionally hunter-gatherers moving from place to place to gather food from plants and hunt prey for meat. Different hunting tools were used including the legendary throwing sticks or boomerangs. These were thrown to strike birds or animals and only some were designed to return to the owner afterwards. Some Aboriginal peoples used spears and a woomera, a wooden stick with a hook at one end which helped extend the throwing range of a spear to distances of over 90m.

Today, boomerangs with intricate painted designs are bought by thousands of tourists.

Aboriginal Culture

Without a written language, Aboriginal culture was passed on to new generations using music, dance, storytelling and art, particularly paintings built up from individual dots of colour. Much of the art and stories concern Dreamtime, a complex set of beliefs about the origins of the world, which is said to have been made by creatures called Ancestors. One of the Ancestors was the rainbow serpent, which burst from the Earth to create streams and rivers.

Aboriginal artist Charles Inkamala paints at the Ngurratjuta Art Centre in Alice Springs.

Song and Dance

Aboriginal gatherings called corroborees are held to celebrate Aboriginal culture and feature music and dance. Those who take part in the ceremonies often wear special body paint made from crushed rocks and soil. Music is provided by the voice, by clapping sticks banged together and by the didgeridoo. This long, hollow tube (often made from a Eucalyptus tree) gives off a deep echoing sound when played expertly.

Adults and children take part in a traditional Aboriginal dance.

Aussie Tucker

Australian tucker (food) ranges from traditional staples, such as fish and chips, to Greek, Middle Eastern and Asian foods – a legacy of the large numbers of immigrants from those regions who have settled in the country. For all the clever cuisine around, an Australian favourite remains the meat pie! This minced beef pie is usually eaten with a big dollop of tomato ketchup. Over 250 million are gobbled up each year.

meat pie

NO WAY!

Some bush tucker (food traditionally eaten in outback Australia), such as quandong fruits and even witchetty grubs, are on sale in some Australian restaurants and supermarkets.

Australian Inventions

Lamingtons are named after the Governor of Queensland from 1896 to 1901.

Australians are proud of their own food inventions which include damper – a yeast-free bread often cooked in fires – and Vegemite, a savoury spread sold in jars or toothpaste-like tubes. Many Aussies have a sweet tooth and like various home-produced 'bikkies' (biscuits) and Lamingtons – square-shaped sponge cakes covered in a layer of chocolate icing and dried coconut. Some dishes, like stir-fried barramundi (a freshwater fish found in Northern Australia) combine Australian ingredients with other cuisines.

Outdoor Eating

With a warm climate and plenty of scenery to admire, it's no surprise that many Australians are barbie bonkers. Many parks around Australia feature barbecues for public use. Typical foods grilled outdoors include pumpkin, chicken, fish, prawns, snags (Aussie sausages) and various cuts of beef. In more recent times, kangaroo, emu and crocodile have been reared for their meat.

Farming

Australia is a massive farming nation and produces much of its own food. Tropical fruits and vegetables are grown in the north of the country and cereal crops, grapes, tomatoes and root vegetables in the south. There are more cattle in Australia than there are people. Around 26 million cattle are reared for beef whilst almost 3 million dairy cows produced 9.3 billion litres of milk during 2011-12. Australia currently has over 68 million sheep, reared for their wool and meat. Many are looked after on giant ranches known as sheep stations.

An Aboriginal jackaroo or "ringer" (cowboy) musters (rounds up) cattle at a cattle station (ranch) in Australia's Northern Territory.

Posing in his Aussie flag apron, a young man barbecues on a boat.

Everyday Life

Australia holds a vast mix of people all knitted together by pride in their country and their outgoing, fun-loving style. Many Aussies have a good sense of humour and form friendly rivalries with people from other Australian states - people from the state of New South Wales, for example, are nicknamed, 'Cockroaches'. Australians often use opposites to describe people like, 'Curly' for a bald man and 'Rowdy' for a quiet person!

NO WAY!

The Beer Can Regatta in Darwin every July or August sees people sail in boats made solely from empty beer cans.

Life and Leisure

Australia is a wealthy country and most of its population enjoy a good standard of living. Leisure time is often spent outdoors, from swimming and eating on the beach to walking, cycling and rollerblading through city parks. Most Australians are conscious of the environment and tend to conserve water when they can by, for example, turning the tap off when brushing their teeth.

Riding the waves on a boogie board is a great way to spend the afternoon!

Many School of the Air children get one or two direct hours of tuition by radio from teachers every day.

School Days

Every kid in Australia gets an education from age 5 to 15-17, even if they don't physically go to school. For children living in isolated parts of the country, there is the School of the Air service which uses radio communications and the internet to teach children at home. The school year starts in late January or early February. High school students usually take their final exams in late November and early December.

Festivals and Holidays

Australia Day is a national holiday and commemorates the arrival of the First Fleet of British settlers to Sydney Cove on 26 January 1788. It's celebrated every year with fireworks, face-painting, flag-waving and a number of music festivals. The Tunarama festival at Port Lincoln, for instance, is held on Australia Day and features competitors hurling tuna fish as far as they can!

Fireworks light up Sydney at the city's massive Australia Day celebrations.

Coming to Australia

Millions of people have left their original countries and made Australia their home. Despite the huge distances from Europe, North America and much of Asia, almost six million people visit Australia every year. Some come to visit relatives. Others come to see the sights and experience the warm climate and traditional Aussie welcome.

Immirants aboard the RMS Zealandic from Liverpool to Australia.

10 Pound Poms ...and Others

After World War II, Brits were offered a one-way ticket to go and settle in Australia for just ten pounds! Thousands took up the offer including the Gibb family – who would become famous as music group, the Bee Gees – and the family of Australia's first female Prime Minister, Julia Gillard, who moved from Wales to Australia in 1966. Thousands of people from other countries – from Italy to Thailand – have also moved to the country. The 2011 Census showed that more than one in four of all Australians were born overseas.

The eyecatching Pinnacles rock formations in Numbung National Park.

Many of Australia's tourists are Australians, keen to visit other parts of their country. Thousands of retired Aussies buy motorhomes to travel around the country for months at a time. In contrast, many foreign tourists are young people and backpackers, who stay at hostels and pick up casual work as they travel round the country. Visitors flock to the country's big cities and beaches, the Great Barrier Reef and get a taste of the outback by visiting towns like Alice Springs.

National Parks

Australia has more than 500 national parks, protected areas of outstanding natural beauty or importance. The country's largest national park is Kakadu which has an area of 19,804km^2 – almost half the size of Switzerland. It features lush wetlands as well as amazing ancient rock carvings and paintings from Aboriginal peoples who have lived in their area for 40,000 years. Many national parks protect areas that are sacred to Aboriginal peoples.

Kakadu National Park boasts abundant birdlife and ancient rock paintings.

More Information

Websites

- http://www.amusingplanet.com/2012/11/the-big-things-of-australia.html
  See a selection of Australia's famous roadside Big Things including a 12-tonne koala and a 17m-high lobster!

- http://www.australia.com
  Home of Tourism Australia on the Web, this site is packed with information and images of Australia's great attractions from Uluru to Sydney's sights.

- http://australia.gov.au/about-australia/australian-story/early-explorers
  Read stories about Australia's early explorers at this massive website, which also has lots more fascinating facts and tales on its About Australia page.

Apps

There's Nothing Like Australia
Available for both Android and iTunes devices, this app from Tourism Australia presents many colourful scenes and videos of the country.

Country Facts: Australia
An app of facts about the country's geography, history and culture.

Australian Sports News
Gives you the latest Australian Football results and much more.

Clips

http://www.youtube.com/watch?v=OqymJpihpPY
Get the lowdown on how Australian Rules Football is played with lots of action clips here.

http://www.youtube.com/watch?v=uW6795YYL5A
Watch a series of traditional dances performed by the Kawanji Aboriginal dance troupe.

www.youtube.com/watch?v=wbNein3vVKM
See the Great Barrier Reef in colourful close-up from *National Geographic*'s underwater cameras.

Movies and TV

Red Dog (PG)
A 2011 family movie based on the true story of a travelling cattle dog in Western Australia.

Wild Down Under
Available as DVDs, these BBC programmes take a close look at the amazing animal life of Australia.

Rabbit Proof Fence (PG)
Three aboriginal girls escape from a camp and cross the outback to get home in the 1930s.

Books

Discover Countries: Australia by Chris Ward
(Wayland, 2013)

Great Barrier Reef by Valerie Bodden
(Franklin Watts, 2011)

Stories from the Billabong by James Vance Marshall
(Frances Lincoln Children's Books, 2010)

Travelling Wild: Sailing the Great Barrier Reef by Alex Woolf
(Wayland, 2013)

Australian film
The Story of the
Kelly Gang (1906)
was the first ever
feature-length film!

Glossary

backpackers Visitors, mostly younger adults, who travel around a country carrying their kit on their back.

census A survey of the population of a country often made by a government to obtain information about the people they govern.

dialect A variation or version of a language spoken by a particular group of people.

exports Goods or raw materials which are sent to another country for sale or trade.

hostels Cheap places to stay overnight for travellers.

immigrants People who move to another country to start a new life.

manufacturing industry Businesses that turn raw materials into finished goods for sale.

Poms Nickname given to British, particularly English, people by Australians.

predators Creatures which hunt and prey on other creatures for their food.

raw materials Substances, such as metals, woods and plastics, which are used to make finished goods.

sacred Considered holy or very important to the religion or beliefs of a people.

venomous A creature that contains a poison it can use to defend itself or disable prey to eat.

wetlands An area of low-lying land which is saturated with water and is usually marshy or swampy.

Index